VOLUME II

PROVERBS

FROM AROUND THE WORLD

ILLUSTRATED · BY

· KATHY DAVIS ·

*Dedicated
to Ben and Katie
with love.*

VOLUME II

P R O V E R B S

FROM AROUND THE WORLD

A mile walked with a

friend

contains only a hundred steps.

ILLUSTRATED · BY

· K A T H Y   D A V I S ·

Great Quotations Publishing Company

Lombard, Illinois • *a division of GREAT QUOTATIONS, INCORPORATED*

Compiled & Illustrated by
Kathy Davis

The sources from which these proverbs were taken have not been acknowledged, as they are often attributable to more than one source and appear in many variations.

Published in the United States by
Great Quotations Publishing Co.
825 E. Roosevelt Rd. • Suite 600 • Lombard, IL 60148

Printed in Hong Kong

ISBN 1-56245-053-0

1 2 3 4 5 6 7 8 9 10

Printing/AK/Year   98 97 96 95 94 93 92

INTRODUCTION

Kathy Davis has given us a second enchanting collection of Proverbs due to the success of her first book *Proverbs from Around the World.* The public has embraced Proverbs for giving to family and friends.

A proverb is a short saying, full of infinite knowledge that has been handed down from generation to generation. Though many of the proverbs reflect the national character of its origin, each saying has universal appeal. Often amusing, the proverbs are rich in imagery. They can be appreciated for their literal impression as well as on a deeper level for their profound meaning.

The sources from which these proverbs have been gathered are not mentioned, as they are derived from many references, often appearing in different variation.

Combining age-old proverbs with colorful and contemporary artwork, the *Book of Proverbs* is a treasure of international humor and insight.

It takes

time

to build a
castle.

· I R I S H   P R O V E R B ·

**Even a lion must defend
himself against the flies.**

GERMAN PROVERB

**Patience is the key of
joy but haste is the
key to sorrow.**

ARABIAN PROVERB

**Whatever I have given,
I still possess.**

LATIN PROVERB

An inch of gold will not
buy an inch of time.

CHINESE PROVERB

Better to idle well
than to work badly.

SPANISH PROVERB

Arrogance diminishes
wisdom.

ARABIAN PROVERB

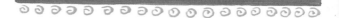

Praise the
children
and they will
blossom.

·IRISH PROVERB·

Up jumps
the
rabbit
where you
least expect it.

· SPANISH PROVERB ·

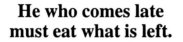

He who comes late
must eat what is left.

YIDDISH PROVERB

To worry about
tomorrow is to be
unhappy about today.

ORIGIN UNKNOWN

Even a small thorn
causes pain.

IRISH PROVERB

**Unshared joy is an
unlighted candle.**

SPANISH PROVERB

**Lights of a thousand
stars do not make
one moon.**

CHINESE PROVERB

**All sunshine makes
a desert.**

ARABIAN PROVERB

One must
lose a
minnow
to catch a
salmon.

· FRENCH PROVERB ·

A bit of
fragrance
always clings
to the hand
that gives you roses.

· CHINESE PROVERB ·

You can only find
out by trying.

GREEK PROVERB

No one is rich
enough to do without
a neighbor.

DANISH PROVERB

Short visits make
long friends.

AMERICAN PROVERB

**If you tickle
yourself, you can laugh
when you like.**

RUSSIAN PROVERB

**He who sows discord
will reap regret.**

ARABIAN PROVERB

**Diligence is the
mother of good luck.**

FRENCH PROVERB

He that will have the

fruit

must
climb the tree.

· G R E E K   P R O V E R B ·

You can't catch trout
with dry breeches.

SPANISH PROVERB

The glory is not in never
failing, but in rising
every time you fall.

CHINESE PROVERB

Words should be
weighed, not counted.

YIDDISH PROVERB

Everyone
can navigate
in
fine weather.

ITALIAN PROVERB.

If each one
Sweeps
before his own door,
the whole street
will be clean.

· Y I D D I S H   P R O V E R B

**The fallen blossom
does not return to
the branch.**

JAPANESE PROVERB

**No gain satisfies a
greedy mind.**

LATIN PROVERB

**No road is long with
good company.**

TURKISH PROVERB

He that chases

two frogs

will catch neither.

· ARMENIAN PROVERB ·

When money speaks,
the truth is silent.

ORIGIN UNKNOWN

He who laughs – lasts.

NORWEGIAN PROVERB

Birds of prey
do not sing.

GERMAN PROVERB

**Live as though
you were to
die tomorrow.**

LATIN PROVERB

**There is no
need like the lack
of a friend.**

IRISH PROVERB

**One can not
learn to swim
in the field.**

SPANISH PROVERB

Trumpet
in a herd of elephants,
bleat
in a flock of goats,
crow
in the company of cocks.

— MALAYSIAN PROVERB.

**Make a bargain before
beginning to plow.**

ARABIAN PROVERB

**That day is lost
on which one has
not laughed.**

FRENCH PROVERB

**All wish to
know, but none
to pay the fee.**

LATIN PROVERB

A
light heart
lives long.

· I R I S H   P R O V E R B ·

To understand your parents' love you must raise children yourself.

CHINESE PROVERB

The shortest answer is in doing.

GREEK PROVERB

You can't have more bedbugs than a blanket full.

SPANISH PROVERB

**It's no use going to
the goat's house to look
for wool.**

IRISH PROVERB

**Nothing is certain but
uncertainty.**

LATIN PROVERB

**The crying cat catches
nothing.**

ARABIAN PROVERB

To possess ideas
is to gather
flowers,
to think
is to weave them
into garlands.

·GREEK PROVERB·

**To know the road
ahead ask those
coming back.**

RUSSIAN PROVERB

**Good bargains empty
our pockets.**

GERMAN PROVERB

**One always has a good
appetite at another's
feast.**

YIDDISH PROVERB

**The riches that are in
the heart cannot
be stolen.**

RUSSIAN PROVERB

**The wish is father to
the thought.**

LATIN PROVERB

**Look before you leap,
for snakes among sweet
flowers do creep.**

GERMAN PROVERB

Celebrations
have to be made,
troubles
come by themselves.

·Y I D D I S H   P R O V E R B·

**They conquer who
believe they can.**

LATIN PROVERB

**The three best friends
and worst enemies: fire,
wind, and water.**

IRISH PROVERB

**A good conscience is a
soft pillow.**

ARABIAN PROVERB

Better a
hen
in the hand
than an
eagle
in the sky.

· Y I D D I S H   P R O V E R B ·

**Many take by the bushel
and give by the spoon.**

GERMAN PROVERB

**He who seeks a
faultless friend rests
friendless.**

TURKISH PROVERB

**God promises a safe
landing but not a calm
passage.**

BULGARIAN PROVERB

**Everything ripe was
once sour.**

LATIN PROVERB

**What would the
cat's son do but kill
a mouse?**

IRISH PROVERB

**Beauty without grace is
a violet without scent.**

ORIGIN UNKNOWN

He who
gives
to me
teaches me
to give.

·DANISH PROVERB·

Rotten wood cannot
be carved.

CHINESE PROVERB

Arrows pierce the body,
but harsh words pierce
the soul.

SPANISH PROVERB

When an apple is ripe
It will fall.

GERMAN PROVERB

**The fish that escaped is
the big one.**

CHINESE PROVERB

**A ragged colt may
make a good horse.**

ORIGIN UNKNOWN

**Your feet will bring you
to where your heart is.**

IRISH PROVERB

Every short
dog
is bold
in the doorway
of its own house.

· I R I S H   P R O V E R B ·

A man shows his
character by what he
laughs at.

GERMAN PROVERB

It is the worst wheel
of the wagon that
screeches the loudest.

SPANISH PROVERB

A friend's eye is a
good mirror.

IRISH PROVERB

When your
horse
is on the brink
of a cliff
it is too late
to pull in the reins.

·CHINESE PROVERB·

It is a rough road that
leads to the heights of
greatness.

LATIN PROVERB

Go home and make
a net if you desire to
get fishes.

CHINESE PROVERB

One thing today,
another tomorrow.

SPANISH PROVERB

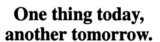

**Listen to the sound of
the river and you will
catch a trout.**

IRISH PROVERB

**A wise man hears
one word and
understands two.**

YIDDISH PROVERB

**Joy and sorrow are
next door neighbors.**

GERMAN PROVERB

As long as the
Sun
shines,
one does not ask
for the
Moon.

· R U S S I A N   P R O V E R B ·

The way in which something is given is worth more than the gift itself.

FRENCH PROVERB

He who prizes little things is worthy of great ones.

GERMAN PROVERB

Well done is half done.

LATIN PROVERB

The journey of a thousand miles starts with a single step.

CHINESE PROVERB

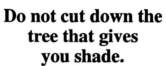

Do not cut down the tree that gives you shade.

ARABIAN PROVERB

When one isn't hungry, all soup tastes sour.

GERMAN PROVERB

However big the
whale
may be,
a tiny harpoon
can rob him of life.

·MALAYSIAN PROVERB·

Much wealth will not come if a little does not go.

CHINESE PROVERB

As the old birds sing, the young ones twitter.

ORIGIN UNKNOWN

The cat catches the bird that sings too early.

GERMAN PROVERB

If you sit
in a hot
bath
you think the
whole town is warm.

· Y I D D I S H   P R O V E R B ·

Speaking without thinking is like shooting without taking aim.

ENGLISH PROVERB

Every time a sheep bleats, it loses a mouthful.

ORIGIN UNKNOWN

A star, however willing, cannot help the moon.

CHINESE PROVERB

He who believes he is deceiving others often deceives himself.

FRENCH PROVERB

When the fox cannot reach the grapes he says they are not ripe.

GREEK PROVERB

It is the quiet pigs that eat the meal.

IRISH PROVERB

Not the cry,
but the

flight

of the wild duck
leads the flock to fly
and follow.

·CHINESE PROVERB·

If you do not sow in the spring you will not reap in the autumn.

IRISH PROVERB

To turn an obstacle to one's advantage is a great step towards victory.

FRENCH PROVERB

Exaggeration is to paint a snake and add legs.

ORIGIN UNKNOWN

**Be good to the child and
he will come to you
tomorrow.**

IRISH PROVERB

**Drop by drop fills
the tub.**

FRENCH PROVERB

**Hidden music counts
for nothing.**

LATIN PROVERB

Make thyself a
Sheep
and the
wolf
is ready.

· RUSSIAN PROVERB ·

**If you stop every time
the dog barks, your road
will never end.**

ARABIAN PROVERB

**By failing we learn
to go safely.**

IRISH PROVERB

**Daylight will peep
through a very
small hole.**

JAPANESE PROVERB

**It is the deed
that matters, not
the fame.**

GERMAN PROVERB

**Overcooked
stew loses its flavor.**

SPANISH PROVERB

**He who rides
the tiger is afraid to
dismount.**

CHINESE PROVERB

It is good
everywhere,
but
home
is better.

· Y I D D I S H   P R O V E R B ·

**If everyone gives a
thread, the poor man
will have a shirt.**

RUSSIAN PROVERB

**A lock is better
than suspicion.**

IRISH PROVERB

**Courage consists
not so much in avoiding
the danger as in
conquering it.**

LATIN PROVERB

**Thinking is the
essence of wisdom.**

PERSIAN PROVERB

**A narrow mind has a
broad tongue.**

ARABIAN PROVERB

**Luck never gives;
it only lends.**

SWEDISH PROVERB

A mile
walked with a

friend

contains only
a hundred steps.

· R U S S I A N   P R O V E R B ·

ABOUT THE ARTIST

Painter, art educator and graphic artist, Kathy Davis brings unique talent and creativity to the Great Quotations product line. Influenced by nature, people and all other forms of art, Kathy's style is light and friendly. Her proverbs combine inspiration and humor to form a contemporary look that makes her work distinctively unique. Kathy lives outside of Philadelphia with her two children, Ben and Katie.